Hints *for* Parents

Hints *for* Parents

by Gardiner Spring, D.D.

with Gospel Encouragements

by Tedd Tripp

Shepherd Press

Main Text © Pat Leahy 2004
Comments © Tedd Tripp 2004
ISBN 0-9723046-6-5

Shepherd Press
PO Box 24
Wapwallopen, PA 18660
www.shepherdpress.com
(800) 338-1445

Cover Layout & Design: Tobias' Outerwear for Books
Interior design and typesetting: Andrew MacBride

Unless otherwise noted, Scripture is taken from the Holy Bible,
New International Version (NIV), © 1972, 1976, 1984 by the
International Bible Society.

Manufactured in the United States of America.

Contents

Recommendations

Preface

"With God's blessing, it is within the power of parents to prevent the decline of piety, suppress common religious error, advance truth and godliness, and reform and save the world." With these powerful words of encouragement, Yale-educated 19th century minister Gardiner Spring steers 21st century parents back to timeless biblical pointers for happy children, happy parents, and happy households.

Look carefully at the construction of human society, and you will be convinced that the religious education of our children is one of God's great means of grace and salvation.

But just where does God's Word and sound experience point us? What will most likely lead to that greatest good, our children's salvation? Here are some hints.

Throughout this book you will find small text blocks in which I have made comments on Spring's *Hints for Parents*.

The text blocks look like this—set off from the main text in italics, and indented on both left and right margins.

Think of my comments like this. Imagine that we are reading this book aloud to each other (I sometimes do this with people I serve as a pastor.). As we read, every now and then, I pause to make some comments and observations that will underscore the importance of what we are reading.

My comments are of various sorts.

Some are reminders of Scripture texts that enhance and deepen the teaching we are reading in Gardiner Spring.

In some cases I am simply holding the hope of the cross before us. We know that all evangelical obedience is motivated by grace and the hope of the gospel, but reminding ourselves of that is necessary lest we fall into a works mentality or legalism.

Some of my comments are designed to show the goodness and validity of things that have long been lost in our culture. The culture has moved at light speed away from foundations in biblical thinking. Spring assumes a framework of culture that was lost generations ago. As God's people part of our calling is to recover what has been lost.

Spring's hints are organized under four headings:

1. Important truths to teach your children.
2. Measures to take to teach these things.
3. Motivations to be faithful in this parental work.
4. Encouragements from the promises of a faithful God.

I am delighted to be reading this book with you. I pray that my comments will enhance our reading and never prove to be a distraction. I think we will find much profit for our souls in Pastor Spring's counsel to us.

Tedd Tripp

CHAPTER ONE

Important Truths to Teach Our Children

Subjection to Authority

Time and again, the Word of God calls us to be in *subjection to authority*. If there is a place where this call should be especially steady and certain, it is the family. And it is a happy family who cultivates this habit of subordination.

The God of nature has assigned the years of childhood and youth to parental control. This wise and generous arrangement simply cannot be upended without jeopardizing the best interests of our children for time and eternity. It is an arrangement that will preserve a child from a thousand evils.

Our presentation of the need for submission or subordination must always be positive. Think of teaching this truth in this manner. "Honey, God, who is good and gracious and kind, who has made you and me and all things for his glory, has given you a Mommy and Daddy. We love you. We have wisdom and life experience. It is good for you to live under God's authority. He has promised (Ephesians 6:1–3) that as you obey, things will go well for you and you will enjoy long life. Mommy and Daddy insist on your obedience because we know it is the best thing for you."

The spirit that considers a parent's wishes, that hesitates to violate a parent's authority; that prefers to sacrifice its own gratification; this spirit is one of the strongest shields that can be thrown around youthful character.

In fact, this spirit of submission helps lead to early purity. Not every dutiful child is pure, but it certainly is more likely that such a child will become so, rather than one of an obstinate, unbending temper.

Sacred Regard for Truthfulness

A *sacred regard for truth* is also a prime habit. What a difference exists in the dispositions of children! Some rarely, if ever, lie and some just seem to be born with a lying tongue. It is terrifying to see how an early habit of extravagant and false storytelling sticks to one's character.

And what a strong barrier this lying throws in the way of holiness and heaven! Children must be taught the immense importance of always speaking the truth. They must see that love, confidence, and honor—or disgust, distrust, and disgrace—will follow them as they let either truth or lies lead them. Every false statement, every art of concealment, every exaggeration, every broken promise only hardens the heart. It burns the conscience and opens another avenue to new seductions.

On the other hand, truth, *pure truth*, with all its simplicity and loveliness, forms the foundation of every moral virtue.

Industrious Habits

Do we have our eyes on our child's best interests? We will prepare them for some sort of useful employment. *Industrious habits* have such a happy influence on the intellectual and moral character. Many a child has been lost to himself, to his family, to the world, and to God, because he had little else to do but indulge himself. But many have been rescued from disgrace and ruin—and pointed toward industry, accomplishment and happiness—simply because they had little time for entertainment.

Our culture does not have a biblical understanding of hard work. Our view is utilitarian; work is what one does to survive or prosper. The truth is that God made mankind to work. Even before the fall of Adam and Eve into sin, they had meaningful work to do. Humanity's calling is to dress and keep the creation. We are to continue the work God has given of understanding, categorizing, and trimming God's creation to make it more beautiful and glorious. Human beings are designed to find fulfillment and joy in meaningful work. When children are never taught about the joys of work, when they are allowed to be self-directed in a life of entertainment and video games, they never enter into understanding the joys of meaningful work for which they were created.

Now, when we talk about hard work, are we enemies of refinement? Certainly not, and we do not want to prepare our children merely for splendid accomplishments. Courtesy and elegance also have a happy influence on character. But combine them with enterprising work habits, and you have a truly powerful force.

Temperance

Temperance is inseparable from a good education. Every generation brings new and different temptations to be intemperate. If a child cannot be temperate, there is little hope that he will be holy or respectable as an adult. Intemperance in thought, word, or deed is simply an indulgence.

For a while an uncurbed, unrestrained child may roll right over life's bumps, but eventually distress and ruin will come calling.

Health, intellect, character, usefulness, comfort, property, conscience, and the soul—all are so easily sacrificed at the shrine of the god of intemperance. A child's mind is the door to his heart, and our children must think, feel, and consider clearly, before they will repent, pray, and love.

If the God of all the earth has appointed parents the immediate guardians of their children's happiness, virtue, and hopes, let us beware how we sow seeds of intemperance in infancy and nurture them in childhood. They are fruitful seeds, and prolific in death.

Selection of Friends

Parents should also consider their children's *selection of friends,* and teach them wisdom in this area. This cannot always be under parental control, but at least we can teach them discernment with regard to their friends.

There are two aspects of this principle. First, the family is the most important set of relationships that God has given us. How we deal with other relationships is directly affected by how we deal with the people in our family.

The second aspect of this principle is recognizing how other people influence and affect us. Idle, vicious, ignorant or skeptical tendencies in our companions often influence us to the detriment of our convictions. We are sometimes unconscious of this effect. Sin is contagious; it seems alright if everyone else is doing it. Children should be encouraged to flee these tendencies, and to live as righteous children of God.

It is here, in the company of older friends, that example persuades, argument encourages, exhortation stimulates, flattery deceives, and ridicule mocks. Here all that is social and sympathetic in a child is pressed into the service of good—or evil.

I often encourage men to consider being downwardly mobile. If taking a job with less stress and responsibility would give you more time at home, make you better able to enjoy your wife and children, and strengthen the development of

nurturing relationships, what could be of greater value? In an interesting juxtaposition, Proverbs 23 (compare verses 4–5 with 24–25) warns against pursuit of riches, which can "sprout wings and fly off," and tells of the delight and great joy of the father of a wise son. Do whatever you must to give yourself to relationships that make home and family attractive to your children. It is a fact of life in 21st century homes that children will find a place to meet their relationship needs. They have access to everything from internet to transportation. Make your home a fun place to be.

"He who walks with the wise grows wise, but a companion of fools suffers harm." (Proverbs 13:20). Many parents have seen their hopes die in such a circle of friends.

Our children's relaxation and even their employment (where possible) should ideally be at home. No matter where they are, their entertainment should never bring reproach upon a well-governed and godly family.

This means that parents may need to deny themselves some creature comforts. Is this unthinkable in our current affluence? If by a few sacrifices you could purchase for your children the habit of loving their home, is any price too high? Those families are best educated, and exhibit the most moral feeling, which are most tenderly attached to home. Soon enough, our children will be extending their borders beyond it.

While we ought not to be completely separated from the world, every family ought to be a little world within itself. A bright, strong affection for the images and friendships of early life so easily draws an affectionate child away from temptations. They bind him to his home, so that no matter how far a child may be removed from your control, as long as this affection moves and glows within him, his love for home will keep him from falling.

One Day in Seven

If there is one fresh lesson for the modern child, let it be the fourth commandment. Let a child be taught to *"remember the Sabbath day, to keep it holy,"* and into what a special sphere of moral influences he is thrown! He is immediately brought nearer the kingdom of heaven. A divine barrier surrounds him. I doubt whether it's possible for such a child ever to be abandoned, without first breaking through the restraints of this sacred day.

Virtuous men think highly of the Sabbath. They know that nothing returns so regularly as does the Sabbath to bless the world. So why would a child be allowed to make light of the obligations of this holy day? Why would he somehow attempt to put himself beyond its joys?

Take on the challenge of making the Lord's Day a special day of enjoyment for the family. Help your children anticipate the day as a time of special worship and wonderful fellowship. Spend the day with Christian friends. Talk about God's good ways. Have special Christian story books to read during the afternoons. Take a hike and let God's creation tell you about his glory. Take advantage of the fact that God has graciously given you one day in seven to devote to spiritual growth and development. Make it a fun day. Celebrate the Sabbath and call it a delight (Isaiah 58:13).

Proper Estimation of the World and Its Culture

What do children esteem most highly? They should be carefully *taught how to estimate this world and its cultures.*

Many prudent, even pious parents encourage far too much zeal for worldly advancement. The spirit of this competitive world is so engrained in our anxious parents' minds. The great object of our pursuit—insensibly—becomes the attainment of wealth and honor.

Certainly parents should be concerned for the character and condition of their children in this life. We want to see our children develop useful and respectable character. We will urge them to unbending fidelity in their profession, whatever it may be. We will inspire our children with a generous love of excellence and a strong desire for good. We will aim for distinction in the best sense of the word.

But it is not an easy matter in everyday life for parents to draw a line between that love of distinction and excellence which the gospel requires, and that which flows from a selfish and worldly heart. We all sin in this regard. It is very natural for us to smile whenever we discover in our children a spirit that is eagerly set on worldly good, or that is simply shrewd. In doing so, we leave them with the impression that, in our estimation, there is no good to be compared with this world.

Do we regularly cultivate higher and nobler principles than the love of earth? If our children are taught that the great business of men is to heap up wealth, attain honors, and enjoy human life, what will be the probable end of their careers? (Colossians 3:23; Matthew 25)

If we would train them up for usefulness and heaven, they must often be reminded to put a low estimate upon every thing beneath the sun. They must not be shielded from the world, but instead taught how vain and empty a thing it is.

The sooner a child can see that there is a higher object of pursuit than his own advancement, that there are more elevated and enduring joys than the sordid and transitory pleasures of time and sense, the sooner he will bear fruit unto eternal life. The sooner he sees that even though he may attain popularity, power and wealth and yet be filled with disappointment and sorrow, the more quickly he is prepared for eternal usefulness.

One of the most delightful callings of parents is to be dazzled by God and share that dazzling vision with their children. Psalm 145:4 speaks of one generation commending the works of God to another. That Psalm goes on to speak of telling of God's glorious majesty and the awesome power of his works. Being dazzled by God is the most soul satisfying delight that human beings can know, but we must confess that it is hard to hold that vision day by day. What an encouragement to know that even in our longing to be caught up with the glory and goodness of God, we do not look inside for power; we look to God. We pray with David, "Show me your ways, O LORD, teach me your paths; guide me in your truth and teach me, for you are God my Savior, and my hope is in you all day long" (Psalm 25:4,5).

Let children be taught that God sent them into the world to do their duty, to fill up their life with usefulness, and thus to honor his great name. If this generous principle takes its seat in their hearts, they will enjoy greater real happiness than if they sit in the thrones of princes, or become possessors of untold millions.

If parents know their children's hearts—and especially if they know their own—they will always tremble for them at the prospect of career advancement. The wisdom that comes from above will lead them often to say to their child, as God did to the Prophet, "Do you seek *great things* for yourself? *Seek them not*" (Jeremiah 45:5).

Let children be taught that God sent them into the world for the sole purpose of obeying him, and bringing honor to his great name. If this principle rests in their hearts, and becomes a controlling influence on their lives, they will find contentment and satisfaction in the work God has given them (Colossians 3:23).

The Apostle Paul reminds us in Romans 1:25 that people make an exchange. We exchange the worship of God for the worship of idols. These idols are not always statuary; they are idols of the heart. Common heart idols are love of possessions, pride and performance, power and influence, pleas-

ure and sensuality. We make an exchange and worship and serve these things in the place of God. Sometimes Christian parents lose their perspective and inadvertently feed the idols rather than help children see that life is found in knowing and loving God. The antidote? Drink deeply from God's river of delights, feast on the abundance of his house (Psalm 36:8), and hold these joys up to your children.

A Generous Spirit

Oh, the lifelong joy and reward of a *generous spirit*!

This is a chord to which the conscience always vibrates. Children quickly grasp this truth: A selfish spirit is a low, abject and mean spirit. There is nothing more elevated, more grand and noble, than a benevolent and disinterested one.

Let your children be taught the evil of a selfish spirit, and the beauty and excellence of a disinterested spirit, unattached to toys of dust. Help them to think of the welfare of others. Form in them the habit of consulting the wishes and feelings of others. Fix their minds upon objects that are great and good.

Prepare them for acts of generosity. Show them that "it is more blessed to give than to receive," that there is more pleasure in offering a favor than accepting it, and more lasting joy in the enlarged, public spirit of the gospel, than the low, groveling spirit of the world.

Children can quickly discover that there are interests greater than their own, and, if they have an enlarged and princely spirit, interests which they will be happier for investigating.

We must guard against the thought that such generosity of character is not possible in our children. It is true that they are "hard-wired" for selfishness. But remember Jesus' words to Peter, "With man this [everything pertaining to salvation] is impossible, but not with God; all things are possible with God" (Mark 10:27). God will take your patient teaching of your children and authenticate its truthfulness to their hearts. Your hope as you teach them to have magnanimity of heart (and model it in your relationships with others) is that God will use His Word to persuade your children of its truth. Your job is to set forth truth plainly; God's job is to shine the light into their hearts. Of course, the most powerful way to teach generosity of spirit and substance is through what you do, not just what you say.

We become great-hearted when we see the great-heartedness of God. Beholding is becoming (2 Corinthians 3:18). Show children the kindness, graciousness, mercy, magnanimity, goodness and generosity of God and this will have a trans-forming influence.

Let their grand inquiry be, not, What interests me?, but What does my duty require? What does generosity require? What does the spirit of kindness and disinterestedness require? What does God require?

∾ ∾ ∾

The 19th century commentator Thomas Scott was well known for his remarkably happy, successful family. When once asked about his method, he replied, "I have always sought for them in the first place, the kingdom of God and his righteousness." Happy parent! Happy children! where the "kingdom of God and his righteousness" take the precedence in every plan and arrangement for human life!

To the religious character of our children, everything else ought to be made subservient. Our high privilege is to "bring up children in the nurture and admonition of the Lord." Whatever others may say or do, Christian parents should choose for their children that "good part which shall not be taken from them." To them, everything else should be like dust.

Exhaust the weight and vigor of your effort here! Our

children are heirs to immortality. They are creatures of responsibility, and are rapidly advancing to the judgment seat. Soon they will be upon a bed of death from which they will ascend to heaven or descend to hell, to the extent they sought or rejected, followed or despised their great Redeemer.

We read something like the paragraphs above and our hearts say, "Yes and amen," to it all. Most of us feel agreement mixed with guilt and a profound sense of our failure. The enemy of our souls is making an assault on us. He is throwing his fiery darts at us. "You can't do this stuff. You are a failure. You are so weak. You might not even be a Christian. It is too late for your kids." His desire is to overwhelm us with our failure and our guilt and fill our thoughts with doubt and unbelief.

We lift the shield of faith against these flaming arrows. And we wield the Sword of the Spirit—the Word of God.

"I am the vine; you are the branches. If a man remains in me and I in him, he will bear much fruit; apart from me you can do nothing" (John 15:5).

"No temptation has seized you except what is common to man. And God is faithful; he will not let you be tempted beyond what you can bear. But when you are tempted, he

will also provide a way out so that you can stand up under it" (1 Cor. 10:13).

"I can do everything through him who gives me strength" (Phil. 4:13).

"His divine power has given us everything we need for life and godliness through our knowledge of him who called us by his own glory and goodness. Through these he has given us his very great and precious promises, so that through them you may participate in the divine nature and escape the corruption in the world caused by evil desires" (2 Peter 1:3,4).

Let us remember that with all our appropriate efforts to have the shaping influences of our child's life be filled with happiness and spiritual substance, it is not those efforts or influences that will save them. That is God's work alone and he delights in showing mercy.

It is painfully true: Ordinarily, children will not become holy without persevering parents. We cannot expect them to become skillful in the arts, learned in the sciences, or useful in the world without our anxious attention. And if we hope to see them become the children of God, they must understand that, in our estimation, their character absorbs and eclipses every other intention of our parental love.

CHAPTER TWO

ℰ

Measures to Take in Teaching Our Children

Set an Example

"Be what you wish your child to be," the saying goes. So much is accomplished by example. It influences children long before instruction can inform, or authority can bind. "Rules constrain; example is alluring. Rules compel; example persuades. Rules are a dead law, example a living law." Next to the law of conscience, example is the first law with which children are acquainted, and it often remains their strongest motive to action after all others are forgotten.

Children are imitative beings, and they quickly understand what they see and hear. The example of an affectionate and watchful parent is a powerful influence. No child is too young to be the accurate observer of its parent's conduct, and to be purified or contaminated, by that example. However unwittingly, we are constantly molding our children's minds, habit, and character by the power of our example.

Who among us desires for our children to be unyielding, overbearing, contemptuous, unkind, unfriendly, or discourteous? But if they discover these in us, our example will govern their conduct.

Perhaps most to the point in this very affluent society: We do not want our children to be afraid of work or hardship, so why do we ourselves pursue fashion and leisure? The message quickly forms in their minds: My parents do not consider hard work, or diligence, or "redeeming the time," to be reputable or pleasurable. They are satisfied with an easy life. With such a message, is it likely that our children will aspire to energy, usefulness and accomplishment?

We want our children to be honorable and completely truthful. We want them to be punctual and thorough. But if they hear us extolling these virtues and know that instead we bend the truth and are disorganized and careless, will not our conduct trump our preaching?

We want our children to carefully choose their friends and conversation. But what if we are careless in this regard? What are the pleasures of modern society? Judging from the reality of the popular market today, they lie somewhere on a spectrum that stretches from popular entertainment to gambling to drunkenness to pornography to prostitution. And now, perhaps more than ever, all of these lie in some form waiting to entice our children. Must we give them an easy opening—right into our own lives and homes?

Example rules. Do we express careless doubts about the truth of God's word and the power of the gospel? Do we not reverence the Sabbath? Do we neglect regular worship? Are we "conformed to this world?" Are we careless about tying ourselves to a body of believers? Is our object to be rich, splendid, and honored by all? If so, will we have any ground for disappointment if our example defeats our instructions?

We are always acting in the presence of our children, so let us do it in such a righteous way that they are tempted to imitate us.

In a simple exhortation to Timothy, Paul underscores the importance of parental example. He says that Timothy should continue in the things he has learned and become convinced of since infancy because he knows those from whom he learned them (2 Timothy 3:14,15). We know that

Timothy had learned sincere faith from his mother, Eunice, and grandmother, Lois (2 Timothy 1:5).

We want to be parents who can say to our children, "Continue in sincere faith because you know those from whom you learned it. Son, you know me, you know that I purposed to live for God's glory. You know I am not perfect, but you know the sincerity of my desire to live for God."

Earlier in the same book, Paul reminds us that we are saved by the power of God who saved us and calls us to holy living, not because of good things in us but because of his own purpose and grace (2 Timothy 1:9). It is this grace that was given to us before all time that gives us hope to be the example we want to be.

Surely we all feel our weakness and neediness. If we look inside for strength to be a consistent good example we will conclude we are like Old Mother Hubbard's cupboard— bare! Praise God that we can be strong in the grace that is found in Christ Jesus (2 Timothy 2:1).

Provide Vigorous Instruction

Children are not merely creatures of imitation, but creatures of intellect. They examine and judge the impressions they get, and confirm or reject them according to how they are taught.

There is no subject off limits for parents in reasoning with their children. What gratification for a child to be convinced and informed! Frequent conversation with your children—not preaching, but familiar conversation—will bear immediate fruit. Your child must feel that you want to inform his understanding and judgment, enlighten his conscience, and impress his heart.

Now, you must recognize a mournful fact: Your child is depraved. You will fail utterly to educate him if you don't recognize this sad reality. He possesses a supremely selfish spirit; self-indulgence is king. Worse, unless he is instructed in moral truth, he will become a slave of low appetites and unholy passions. He will become a giant in wickedness.

But the Creator has given this child a tender conscience. Enlightened, it differentiates between right and wrong and gives him a sense of obligation; it is how a child becomes a moral agent and different from an animal. He can learn that he is a responsible creature. Does he know his relationship to God? He must feel accountable to him.

What a man ought to know, he ought to begin to know very early. The great moral principles, which enlighten his adult conscience and character, ought to penetrate and work on his dark mind in childhood.

What God requires of parents is clearly spelled out: "And these words which I command you shall be in your heart, and you must diligently teach them to your children, when you walk, when you lie down, and when you rise up." And not just principles. Children must be taught the truth about God: His being, perfections, and government; redemption by Jesus Christ, the influence of the Holy Spirit, the beauty of true faith, the joys and honors of an unreserved devotion to Jesus, his precious promises for the godly and the awful terrors awaiting the ungodly.

All of life instructs our children. Whether it is formal or informal instruction, it tells our children how to interpret life and how to respond—the two great occupations of life.

There are many excellent ways of holding biblical truth before your children. Some are mentioned in this section of Hints for Parents. *As you hold biblical truth before your children, you do so in the knowledge that God's truth is powerful and self-authenticating. The prophet Isaiah uses this wonderful word picture in chapter 55 of his prophecy. He says the word of God is like rain and snow that does not return to the heavens without watering the earth and making it bud and flourish. The word of God, Isaiah says, is like that, it accomplishes God's good purposes (Isaiah 55:10–13).*

We know that God works through his word. He makes his revealed truth accomplish his great redemptive purpose. Isaiah goes on to say that he does this for his own fame and renown. What a great comfort and encouragement for you as you use the word of God in the lives of your children! God will work through his word. You can find solid hope there.

Instruction in God's word should be systematic, regular and frequent. It should be casual, too ("When you walk by the way"). Early let them be made familiar with Scriptures. Let their memories be stored with its history, its biography, and its truths. Let them also be stored with easy and familiar catechisms, prayers, and sacred hymns. How tragic that these ancient tools have fallen into disuse! Let a child's attention constantly be diverted from light and destructive reading, to that which is profitable and constructive.

Who disagrees today that the great bulk of literature and entertainment exerts a destructive influence, both on the intellectual and moral character? But let us not just curse the darkness. Let children be committed to teachers who will exert a holy influence on their youthful minds. Let this influence charm and win them to the love of virtue and godliness. In this furnishing of their minds, let them be so preoccupied with the best furniture, that they shall have little room for noxious and polluting guests.

In conversing with them on the great subject of their soul's salvation, we should address them with all affection and tenderness. Let us urge and plead with them to flee from the "wrath to come." We want them to see that this is a subject about which we feel the deepest and most tender concern. This a subject that brings tears to our eyes, and persuasion from our tongues. On this matter all the passion and strength of our affection flows forth in "thoughts that glow, and words that burn."

There is an inexcusable backwardness in many parents when it comes to conversing on religious subjects. Do we pile religious conversation onto our children, no matter how inappropriate the timing or application? Every opportunity for instruction should be well timed, and never made tedious.

Timing is everything. In the history of a child, there are seasons of embarrassment and tenderness, and there are seasons of openness. And there are times when we ourselves think much, feel deeply, and pray earnestly, for the salvation of our children. Out of these special times, we may proceed with special confidence and a delightful fullness of soul, to serious and heartwarming conversations with our children (with more than usual hopes of success)!

As you pray for wisdom in discerning these seasons in the lives of your children, encourage yourself with Philippians 1:9–11. "And this is my prayer: that your love may abound more and more in knowledge and depth of insight, so that you may be able to discern what is best and may be pure and blameless until the day of Christ, filled with the fruit of righteousness that comes through Jesus Christ—to the glory and praise of God."

These things that you so deeply need—love, knowledge, insight, discernment, purity, blamelessness and righteousness—are qualities of character and life that come from God. Don't allow yourself to despair of ever reflecting these qualities. Join in Paul's prayer that they might abound in your life. Pursue them in the knowledge that God is able to make these graces abound in your life.

This is a job for parents alone. Here, the faithful efforts of a faithful father, and even more, a godly mother, are most important. Faithful parents certainly owe much to the other faithful adults in a child's life: Sunday school teachers, nannies, and godly women and elders in Christ's church. These all have obligations that may never be forgotten.

But that parent who leaves her child only to the instruction of teachers, or father who neglects the Christian education of his family at home (because he can shift the burden onto a religious school) has not carefully considered his responsibility. More importantly, he underestimates the power a parent has in shaping the character and destiny of his children.

Gain Their Confidence

In all their conduct toward them, parents should seek to gain children's confidence. Every child should be convinced that his parent is his best friend. He must know that there are none on whose devoted attachment he may so completely rely. There are none who will do and suffer—so patiently and so long—for him. Who look for no higher gratification or reward than his good conduct and highest welfare.

Once we plant these thoughts in a child's heart, we cannot fail to have a strong hold upon his conscience and character.

But this alone may not gain their confidence. We should use every sensible and lawful means to secure the affections of our children, to induce them to choose our company, to enter into conversation with us without embarrassment, and trust us with their own private affairs.

In 1 Thessalonians 2:7–11, Paul the Apostle uses the intimacy of the mother/child and father/child relationship to describe his shepherding as a gospel minister. Paul's use of parent/child relationships as a paradigm for pastoral care shows God's intention for parents.

Mothers are described in this passage as gentle, sharing their very lives because of the preciousness of their children. Fathers are described as inspiring conduct that ennobles — encouraging, comforting and urging children to live in a manner that is worthy.

Paul says this kind of conduct, marked by gentleness and gracious exhortation, is holy, righteous and blameless. This kind of conduct toward our children is not just wishful thinking for us. God's grace in us generates "work produced by faith, labor prompted by love, and endurance inspired by hope in our Lord Jesus Christ"(1 Thessalonians 1:3). God's grace has been given to us to make us like this.

Remember, influence is far more powerful than authority as children transform from the dependent and easily-directed early years to the self-aware years, with the heady realization of the world and all of its possibilities.

Children who want to be respectful to their parents are sometimes afraid of becoming too familiar. And some parents who desire to be respected and honored by their children strangely resist such familiarity.

Where children are held in slavish fear, the fault is always the parent's. Even with children whose tempers seemingly cannot be controlled by other means, there is little hope of having any happy, long-term influence as long as they are held in the bondage of fear.

Gaining the confidence of an impetuous child—while restraining him—is no small feat. It calls on all the kindness, discretion, and firmness of a godly parent, who will soon throw up his hands—to the Father of lights!

Train Your Children to Be Under Authority

The great question in every act of parental discipline is, what will be for the best good of the child? Where a family is small, and especially where there is but a single child, this may be the only question.

Every good system of education maintains a kind and wholesome authority. The policing of a family is of a peculiar kind, and its great operating principle comes from the Apostle Paul: "Fathers, do not provoke your children to anger, but bring them up in the nurture and admonition of the Lord."

To be what it ought to be, your authority must be absolute. "Those who maintain the strictest discipline, give the fewest strokes." If your authority is absolute, it need not be severe. Your will should first be righteous, and then it should be law. Anything to which you cannot freely consent, should be considered as altogether out of the question for your child.

The statements in the above paragraph strike our 21st century ears as harsh and extreme. They must be seen through the lens of what follows about mild and affectionate parenting that is truly kind.

What Gardiner Spring is asserting here is the necessity for your parenting to be clear and consistent. Whatever is truly righteous must be the standard in our homes. We cannot give consent for anything that is wrong or unrighteous. We will not serve our children well if we indulge them by allowing, even in moderation, that to which "you cannot freely consent."

I am surprised in speaking with parents who say, "I don't like these video games, but . . ." I usually respond, "If you are convinced they are not good for your children, why not sit down with them and explain your convictions?" I used to say to my children, "I have sought to persuade you of the wisdom of my convictions on this matter. Now, what do you expect of me? You surely would not ask me to deny my conscience in this matter and allow you to do what I believe to be potentially destructive to you. I must ask you to respect my decision."

The inflexibility that Spring calls us to in this section can be gentle and gracious. The Proverbs remind us that "a gentle tongue can break a bone" (Proverbs 25:15).

We are witnessing everywhere around us the bleak alternative to Spring's counsel. In our culture children are their own decision making authorities to their own detriment and ruin.

Family government must never be impulsive. Do you exercise your authority only when the notion strikes you? Are you foolishly indulgent? Is your authority so various and changeable that your children don't know where to "find" you? Do you announce a rule and then, without any change of circumstance, revoke it? Such government does not deserve the name. It is enough to spoil any child in the world.

It is hard to over-emphasize the importance of children taking their place under parental authority or the absolute ne-

cessity that parental authority represent the mighty and merciful God in every aspect. In our culture people either tend toward indulgent tenderness or demanding authoritarianism. One makes the child's desires supreme, the other makes the parent's demands supreme. What God calls us to is authority that is truly gracious and kind.

A mild, affectionate government is the most authoritative, so your authority ought to be exceedingly kind. Children are naturally displeased, even angry, when governed, but they ought to find no foothold for their anger in their parents' behavior. The human heart revolts at simply being restrained, and all that much more when authority is rash and unkind. Weave in your kindness with every act of discipline, and your government will rarely fail to influence.

By the time a child can walk—and even earlier—he should be taught implicitly to obey.

If parental authority is not established early, it will never be established. When I say early, I mean very early. By the time a child is 15 years old, authority—bare authority—will not reach him. He must then be under a government of influence, or be self-governed, or not governed at all.

The alternative is simply more difficult and impractical! This early habit of subjection, even to impatient and unbending children, will soon become easy, and parents will find it effective too.

Here may I add: I have no doubt of the propriety and importance of corporal punishment. God has abundantly approved of it in his word. But it is only for a child. When that child passes from childhood to, say, fifteen years of age, the same rod does him injury (unless it is used in response to downright impudence or disobedience). If he will not be governed by reason, kindness, influence, he needs a stronger arm than the discipline of his family.

In our day when children are "adultified" very early and quite sophisticated in their ideas, most parents will find that the rod is most effective in dealing with young children. As children get older they get more stoic about the rod. What it would take to make the same impression on a 13 year old that one makes on a 3 year old would require a very severe beating. Generally, spanking will be reserved for young children.

Indeed, all our efforts to train up our children in the way they should go exhaust their influence before we are aware of it. The days of childhood—these are the seasons when character is formed. And if these are neglected, it will be a miracle of mercy if our children are not lost.

Parents' purpose in discipline should never come in collision with each other. Marital discord is the deadliest foe to the education of children. On every topic of education, let there be no jarring between the united head of a family.

Are you, for example, a proponent of extravagant leisure and entertainment, and your spouse opposed? Are you "early to bed, early to rise," and your spouse up at all hours? Is your spouse firm in authority, and you chide her as severe, and the enemy of your children's pleasures? Your bone of contention is the child you love! Who can wonder if your authority and your child are sacrificed in the broil?

When should parental government cease? Wisdom would tell you to look at the disposition of your child, and the condition of your family. Are you seeing increasingly joyful experiences with your children? That would certainly point in the direction of their freedom.

On the other hand, if your experiences are bitter, patience—not harsher government—is the remedy. Patience, and hope in God.

— ∽ —

*The temptation in dealing with teenagers who are resisting
our authority is to become more authoritarian. The Bible
gives us wonderful counsel in 2 Timothy 2:24–26. "The Lord's
servant must not quarrel; instead, he must be kind to everyone, able to teach, not resentful. Those who oppose him he
must gently instruct, in the hope that God will grant them
repentance leading them to a knowledge of the truth, and
that they will come to their senses and escape from the trap
of the devil, who has taken them captive to do his will."*

*The battle for your teenagers is not fought through your
power plays. It is fought through a kind and teachable spirit.
It is waged as you turn away from the temptation to re-
sentment. Your weapons are gentle instruction and hoping
in God. These will disarm rebellion.*

*Ultimately, you must recognize that in all your efforts at
child-rearing, you are at the mercy of God. Your children
will never come to faith in Christ because you got everything
right in the child-rearing department. If they come to know
and love God, you will stand in awe of a God who has mercy
on children even though their parents fail.*

*Why do we work so hard at being good parents? We do so
because God is pleased to use the means of our labors to work
his sovereign purposes in the lives of our children. But ultimately
we recognize that it is God's work, not ours, to save our children.*

Nothing will move us to call out to God for his grace to make us tender and to work within our children like a hardy realization that it is grace that will bring our children to Christ.

The profound need of your teens is repentance, knowledge of the truth and coming to their senses. Meet this problem through prayer, hoping in God. Remember, Proverbs 16:21, 24 tells us that pleasant words are a honeycomb; they promote instruction. Children, even teens, cannot resist unconditional love and humility in the authorities they oppose.

Humble, persevering prayer will accomplish much in educating your children. Is your pride not concentrated in your children? Parents of great intellect and determination—especially young parents—are very apt to place great confidence in their own skill, management, and firmness. This pride in our children, and confidence in ourselves will meet with severe trials. The Lord of heaven and earth holds both in his hands.

God means for us to renounce our self-confidence and feel our dependence on him. When we fail—as certainly we will to some extent—we will lie prostrate on our faces and carry our children to the God of all grace and power.

The sooner, more earnestly, and more submissively we do this, the more reason we have to hope.

Parental tenderness is the most pure, the most faithful, and the most energetic, when prayer nourishes it. It is at God's mercy seat that a parent's love all flows out. And God reveals his mercy exactly as our children need it.

The sacraments point us so well to God as the only refuge for our offspring. For many parents, this is the point at which they see most clearly their weakness and God's strength. This is where their faith gets exercised, and once they see it happen, they never let go. When oppressed with disappointment, they can still appeal to the promises of God in this regard.

Let your children hear you pray daily. Pray for them so they can hear you asking God's special blessing on them. Let them hear this passion expressed in the church, by you and by others, so they can know something of their special relationship to God's visible kingdom. And then remember them in your private devotions. An affectionate and faithful parent will not let the Angel of the Covenant go until he blesses his children.

Finally, do not be content to plead only for God's restraining grace! Go on in confidence to ask him for his saving mercy. Plead for them in their sinfulness, lost without Christ's blood. Plead for them because they possess indisputable, inalienable immortality. Plead for them with the tenderness of Jesus. Plead for them with the assurance that someday you will say with Jesus, "Of those which you have given me, I have lost none."

CHAPTER THREE

Motivations for Faithful Parenting—What Will Make You Do It?

The Intrinsic Importance of Every Child

First, the intrinsic importance of every child. The poorest, the weakest, the simplest child, is born for immortality. This value outweighs the entire material universe, no matter how small a mark this child makes on it. The tiniest infant owns a deathless intellect, and is as immortal as the Father of spirits. No one can tell what this child will become.

Moses, Solomon, Mary and Paul were once children. The millions now bowing before God's throne, and other millions looking up from hell, were once children. During their short lives, many of their minds became powerfully active, their views were quickly and astonishingly enlarged, and their vast knowledge enriched generations to come.

But now, in heaven, even the simplest child stands before God knowing more, feeling more intensely than any of the great intellects of this earth. The soul of a child can hold so much. This little, immortal spirit is capable of enjoying (or suffering) more than all intelligent creatures, on earth and in heaven, have yet enjoyed or suffered. Who can help but be overwhelmed at the unfathomable importance of the most "ordinary" child?

You have seen a child die, and just then you know how extraordinarily important and eternal they are. They are torn from you, but you know that this is not a period on their existence. You know in this moment that they have been transmitted from a narrow dungeon to the wide empire of eternity. Fit for heaven, they now have a perfect guardian. They are no longer mortal, but immortal. No longer ignorant, but sensible and significant beyond our comprehension. "Out of the mouths of babes you have ordained praise."

What truths will enable you to carefully devote yourself to this work God gives you to do? Ultimately, it is the truth of amazing grace that motivates us to obedience. In Titus 3, the

Apostle Paul reminds Titus of the kindness and love of God our Savior. He talks to us about the washing of rebirth and renewal by the Holy Spirit, about justification by grace and being full of the hope of eternal life. Then he tells Titus to stress these things so that "those who have trusted in God may be careful to devote themselves to doing what is good."

Think about it. The reminders of your child's immortality must be understood in light of the grace and mercy that God has shown to you and me who are sinners. Grace motivates obedience. Embrace the truths Gardiner Spring brings to you in this section in light of the unspeakable kindness God has shown to you. It will move you to devote yourself to untiring devotion to what is good.

Eternal matters of unknowable magnitude are entrusted to you! Can you view your children not as mere children, but see them in the full manhood of eternity? You are educating a youthful prince. You are molding the character of a princess born for a great empire, who herself may mold the character of millions. Their character will bear the mark of your gracious watchfulness up to the throne of God. Or (may He forbid it) they will carry the evidence of your negligence as they live with the damned!

*What a powerful hedge this reality should be against living
a "form of godliness that denies its power." The gospel of grace
through faith in Jesus Christ alone must inhabit our homes.*

They Call You Father and Mother

They call you father and mother. In spite of their child-
ishness and youthfulness, they prize this tender relationship. They are not orphans, or strangers for whom
nobody cares, who finally wander to their graves without hearing one expression of parental love. They are
your children, your possession! They have this God-
authored relationship with no one else.

"Did he not make *one*? Yet had he the residue of the
Spirit. And wherefore one? That he might seek a godly seed."
Does modern man understand the guilt of trifling with sacred marriage vows? Does he consider the brazen evil of
sending out carelessly conceived, fraudulent offspring? The
man or woman who infringes on God's moral arrange-
ments makes sport of the best interests of society—right
now. So why should we have high hopes for future generations while addicted to base and unholy indulgences?

The God who created, sanctified and blessed the marriage covenant, who "set the lonely in families," has com-

mitted to us the jewels from which he means to adorn his crown. When the God of heaven says, "Take this child, and nurse it for me," how tender an obligation!

Are your children frail? No doubt you passed it on to them. Are they imperfect? How strongly they resemble you! Are they so peculiar they embarrass you? Look inward. Are they immoral? How very likely it is that you have created them in your own image!

You will not stand idly by as someone else listens to their woes, or binds their wounds, will you? A wild ostrich, which has no wisdom, leaves her eggs where they can be crushed. Depraved humans have sacrificed their children to false gods, burning them on the white hot hands of Moloch. Would you do ten thousand times worse by neglecting the heart of your child?

You have the wonderful opportunity of engaging the heart and imagination of your children. Take your children into your confidence as you find grace and strength in Christ day by day. Let them see you as a prayerful person of humble weakness before a God of strength. Nothing will provide your children with an understanding of the power of the gospel like your love and dependence on God.

Another important aspect of spiritual leadership is com-

municating an accurate picture of the world to your children. Your children need to understand the nature of reality. Help them understand that underneath this world of sight and sound there is an unseen world of spiritual reality that gives meaning to the world we see and touch and handle. The tree in the backyard that provides nesting for the birds and squirrels and a place for children to climb and even to build a tree fort, exists at the will of the unseen God. It is his creation; it exists as a hymn of praise to his creativity, wisdom and skill. He has given it to us to enjoy that we might know about him and worship and enjoy him. Your children cannot understand the tree truly without glimpsing in the seen what is unseen.

Helping children understand the nature of reality requires imagination. Our children must see what is unseen. Christians are people whose commitment to the unseen world of spiritual reality dictates our interpretation and response to what we see with our eyes.

The word imagination is not used in Deuteronomy 6, but the use of imagination is essential. Your son will come to you and ask, "What is the meaning of these ceremonies and rituals and rules that we follow?" (Deuteronomy 6:20). To answer this question, you must engage your son's imagination about events in the past, about slavery in Egypt and bold, dramatic deliverance by the outstretched arm of God. Biblical narratives are tangible illustrations of God's Covenant promise, "I will be your God and you will be my holy people."

Engaging the imagination of your children will open their spiritual eyes to what is invisible.

Our Children Are the Next Generation

One generation goes, and another comes. In a few years, our children will be agents of change. They will be at the heart of all that is interesting in the church and the world. Our sun sets, theirs rises. They will be taking our place in the work force and business, and they will have our authority. They must increase and we must decrease.

The world presents itself to them as an unformed mass, a piece of wax awaiting their stamp. They must anticipate its needs. The impression the world then receives will be admired or abhorred for generations to come.

This, then, is the interesting time in the life of a child. This is when impressions are made, when there are few obstacles and little bitterness. Cares are few, imagination is vivid, memory magnetic, and emotions tender. A child's character is accessible by a thousand avenues now that will be closed later.

If our children are educated in the fear of the Lord, the happy influence will extend through many generations, far and wide throughout the earth. When all the rest of the world was pagan, it was through the religious education of Abraham's family that the Jewish nation became a holy nation.

If, on the other hand, this "nurture and admonition of the Lord" is ignored, we need not look far to see the results. Then our only hope is to reform a corrupt world, and that task begins in the family.

Look ahead, and see what part your children will act. What positions will they hold? It depends entirely upon you whether they grow happily accustomed to moral principle, and become friends of virtue and godliness.

What you are doing each day as you live with your children is presenting a picture of reality. You are showing them that you believe that God is good and that he rewards those who seek him. You are telling them each day by loving God and loving others that the law of God is good. As you make a priority of worship you tell them that life is found in knowing and honoring God. When you are kind to people who are unkind, you show the magnanimity and kindness of God. Everything you do and says tells a story to your children. It is important that the story you tell is true.

God Is a Rewarder of Those Who Seek Him

You need to know that this is not all wishful thinking. God has always encouraged parents with real promises and real providence. Right from the start, of course, our parents had better ideas, so the sentence of death was handed down. But look through history at families and nations who have trusted the Lord, or who have even passively felt the influence of Christianity, and compare it to those who have not. You will quickly see the favorable and encouraging influence of this principle.

"I know Abraham, that he will command his children and his household after him; and they shall keep the way of the Lord, to do justice and judgment, that the Lord may bring upon Abraham that which he hath spoken."

Or: "O that there were such an heart in them, that they would fear me, and keep my commandments always, that it might be well with them and with their children forever!"

Or: "The mercy of the Lord is from everlasting to everlasting upon them that fear him; and his righteousness unto children's children."

Or: "The just man walks in integrity; his children are blessed after him."

Or: "The generation of the upright shall be blessed."

Or: "I will pour water upon him that is thirsty, and

floods upon the dry ground; I will pour my Spirit upon
thy seed, and my blessing upon your offspring."

Speaking of his people, God says, "As for me, this is
my covenant with them, says the Lord; my Spirit that is
upon thee, and my words which I have put in thy mouth,
shall not depart out of the mouth of thy seed, nor out of
the mouth of thy seed's seed, says the Lord, from hence-
forth and forever. They shall not labor in vain, nor bring
forth for trouble; for they are the seed of the blessed of
the Lord, and their offspring with them."

Or: "Train up a child in the way he should go, and
when he is old he will not depart from it."

Or: "The promise is unto you, and your children."

Or: "Believe on the Lord Jesus Christ, and thou shall
be saved, and thy house."

God's grace and providence recognizes the obligations
and blessing of this very special tie of parent and child.
The God of Abraham "blesses obedient children for the
sake of their obedient parents." He has a method for trans-
mitting true religion from one generation to another. He
has a scheme for continuing his church in the world. He
has a plan to train up his people for heaven. It is un-
avoidably this: The children of holy parents are placed
solidly within his gracious economy, in his divine government of this world.

The classic passage on this calling is Deuteronomy 6. Through Moses God gave parents a long-term vision in this passage. His focus is not survival or even getting through the week. The callings of spiritual leadership are so that (verse 2) you and your son and your son's son may know and fear the Lord. This three-generation vision will help you resist the temptations to fall into the expediencies of the moment. As parents, we have bigger concerns than the moment; we are concerned with where our grandchildren will be fifty years from now.

Christian families are the nurseries of the divine kingdom. Some may object, pointing out that children of faithful parents are no more sanctified than the children of others. This simply has no basis in reality. Look around society and see that those who give evidence of true faith are—in large part—the children of the faithful. In this regard, it is so important to take a longer view, to look down the halls of time. It is utterly untrue that children of holy parents are as bad as other persons.

Ultimately your hope for your children is not in your abilities or performance, but in the power of the gospel. They are

part of a fallen race of creatures. They need the good news of the gospel that you hold out for them every day. The gospel is powerful. It is self-authenticating. It is suited to their needs as fallen creatures. You can, therefore, live in the hope that it will be the power of God to salvation in the lives of your children.

True, not all children of holy parents are holy. It is likely that not all Abraham's children were. We know for certain that David's were not, and we know some of this can be chalked up to parental unfaithfulness. But we must also acknowledge that the God of all the earth reserves certain rights to himself. We can see why his promises regarding our children are general and indefinite—not definite and particular. Parents would abuse them. Children would too, resting their hopes on their parents alone.

None of this erodes this precious encouragement: Holy parents should expect their children to be holy—and happy. Or this fearful terror: Unholy parents should expect their children to be unholy—and unhappy.

Can a mother forget her nursing child, that she should not have compassion on the son of her womb?

If a son asks bread of him who is his father, will he give him a stone?

The all-wise Governor of the world has entrusted the holiness and happiness of children to us. By what more powerful inducement could he govern a world of families, than this?

CHAPTER FOUR

Courage! Take Courage!

Do Not Get Weary in Well Doing

God's time for the conversion of your children may not be your time. Your efforts may seem to be in vain—even for years—but you will likely at last see your children rejoicing in the graces and comforts of holiness.

He who goes forth and weeps, bearing precious seed, shall doubtless come again with rejoicing, bringing his sheaves with him.

A hardened, ungrateful child may break your heart ten thousand times. He may turn you grey with grief, even to the grave, but you can look back on God's faithfulness and know that you were not negligent in trusting his promises.

One of the liberating results of acknowledging your spiritual need and weakness as a Christian is the help you can get from others. If we recognize that we are sinners, redeemed sinners, but sinners still, and if you live in the truth of your justification, knowing that God has accepted you for Jesus' sake; then you can be open to the help of Christian brothers and sisters.

It is a wonderful thing to drop your guard and say to others who love you and have wisdom and biblical understanding, "Look, I am trying my best to do what God has called me to, but I am weak and my own sins, that I am blind to, get in my way. I need your help."

This is a sign of holiness. Can you hear with joy the corrections and advice of Christian brothers and sisters who have gone before you in this effort? Are you regularly teaching your children to read God's holy word? (Do you read it?) Are you instructing them in the great, eternal truths of Christianity? Do you pray with them, for them, and teach them how to pray? (Do you pray?)

Be a Correctable Parent

You may be doing all of this faithfully, and your children will long praise you for it. But if you know you have been unfaithful in this, know also that this unfaithfulness greatly displeases God. You will feel the bitter consequences forever. Yes, he may allow your children to live out grandly unholy lives before your eyes. You may even live to see them plunge down to death and hell.

Do you stand between God and his blessing for your children? I have simple advice: Reform at once. Take your child by the hand—while you can—and walk them in the paths of holiness and salvation.

Look at your children. Look at their cradle. Anticipate their progress through this ensnaring world. Look at death and judgment. Will you meet them there—with joy? Will you on the morning of resurrection greet your sons and daughters with a smile?

Children—Consider Your High Obligations

Honor your father and your mother, that your days may be long upon the land which the Lord your God has given you.

We have seen this promise delightfully fulfilled. And, tragically, we have seen its implied threat executed with force. In New York, this guilty metropolis, where popular trends and fashions are their most powerful, I have seen so many youth glide down the dangerous current, and I have seen them pay the ultimate price as they scorned authority.

Children, obey your parents in the Lord, for this is right. But I want so much more from you. I want your hearts, your lives, and your existence for him who made you and bought you with his blood.

Remember now your Creator in the days of your youth. Seek the Lord while he may be found, call upon him while he is near.

Hear me once more, if you still despise this great salvation: What is this great infatuation that drives you on to ruin and despair? Tell me it is not just my imagination. Are you sporting with that over which the saints in glory weep? Were you nurtured in the lap of holiness only for the society and employment of fiends? Let the world of darkness never rejoice that you, the object of so many prayers and tears, have become its own child.

The Duty of Catechetical Instruction

by Archibald Alexander, D.D.

In an era like ours when formal catechetical instruction is nearly non-existent, articles like this one from Archibald Alexander are a breath of fresh air and a necessary corrective to our neglect of formal training.

The thing that will move your catechizing beyond the memorization of theological truth will be your life of faith day by day. The children will learn more powerfully the meaning of the words that say we should "glorify God by loving him and keeping his commands" as they see you love him and keep his commands. The value of the Catechism will increase as it finds joyful expression in your life.

This article was originally published in 1837 by the Presbyterian Board of Publication.

Catechetical instruction—oral teaching—was part of everyday life in the first human family.

The First Man surely delivered a stock of important ideas to his children, and they again to theirs, with different degrees of ability and accuracy.

The usual place of instruction was, for a long time, the home. Here the pious patriarch would spend much time dealing out to his listening children the lessons he learned in his youth from his parents, and those learned from his own experience. This form of instruction was known as *catechizing*, which means " oral communication of knowledge."

As long as these parents faithfully performed their duty, they were dispelling the darkness of ignorance and idolatry. As soon as they let it fall into disuse, error and vice almost certainly followed.

God even "certified" Abraham for this kind of teaching: "For I have chosen him, so that he will direct his children and his household after him to keep the way of the Lord by doing what is right" (Genesis 18:19).

God, by Moses, insisted on this duty more than others: "These commandments that I give you today are to be upon your hearts. Impress them on your children. Talk about them when you sit at home and when you walk along the road, when you lie down and when you get up" (Deuteronomy 6:6, 7).

And the Psalmist said, ". . . he commanded our forefathers to teach their children, so the next generation would know them . . ." (Psalm 78:5, 6).

The word *catechize* comes from a Greek verb meaning "to instruct with the voice." In English the word has somehow acquired a narrower meaning: "instruction by question and answer." The Greek word, however, includes *all* kinds of elementary and oral instruction, and it would be nice to bring back the word to its original meaning.

Whatever the case, Scripture seems to fully recognize this mode of instruction, even as it requires the preaching of the word. Indeed, if elaborate and lengthy sermons were our only means of teaching the truth, very little information would make its way into the hearts of the young and the ignorant.

Preaching assumes—and requires—some preparatory knowledge in the hearers if it is going to be useful. Children need to learn in another way.

Viva voce. The apostles and first teachers of Christianity busied themselves, going from house to house giving religious instruction. We know that in the early church children were carefully *catechized* by a course of familiar teaching.

In every church there was a class of *catechumens*, which formed a kind of school. Here the first principles of religion were taught, and early creeds, sacred Scripture, and other Christian doctrine were committed to memory.

Some of these schools became very famous, with teachers of highest character and intellect teaching doctrine and piety. Lovers of sacred literature from all over the known world frequented them. In Alexandria, Egypt, the great teacher Origen was taught at one of the most famous schools, and later became a teacher there.

Until darkness spread over the church, and her unnatural pastors deprived the people of the Scriptures, the church was, as it ever should be, like a great school. Here holy men of God devoted their time to instruction of the rising generation, and of converts to the faith.

In catechetical instruction, the grand secret was—and remains—"A little at a time, repeated often." Whoever would successfully teach children and ignorant adults must not attempt to crowd too many things into their minds at once. It is as preposterous as trying to make a body fit and vigorous by cramming the stomach with as much food as it can hold!

And first truths should be as simple as possible. Tender minds must not be fed with strong meat, but with pure milk. This is the most difficult stage of education—and the most important.

The Bible begins with historical facts, and this should be how religious instruction should begin. It is no small matter that children tend to quickly absorb this type of knowledge. At a very early age, though, moral and doctrinal instruction of the most important kind can be grafted onto the scriptural facts.

Children, we admit, do not completely understand doctrinal catechisms. But it does them no harm to commit these profound words to memory. Will it not be much better to have their young minds stored with salutary truths than with empty or injurious memories? Later, the memory of a catechism can be of utmost value when a person is grasping for a core truth, or when he has no other immediate doctrinal touchstone, or simply no means of correct information.

The old custom of devoting Sunday evening to catechizing children ought to be revived. If church services take up that time, we can easily find an hour another evening for this important work. It is as useful to parents as to children.

Now, these family instructions should be conducted

with great seriousness and kindness, made with affection and tenderness. Chiding and scolding should be avoided.

Let other people exceed us in philosophical speculations and in knowledge of worldly matters. Let us be known for a correct and thorough knowledge of the truths of scripture and the lively doctrines of the church. Surely these truths may not necessarily restrain a person from open sin, but even then the force of the truth often makes itself felt. Knowing the truth, the offender is much more likely to be convinced of the error of his ways.

Later, when the mind falls under serious influence of religious teaching of all kinds, truths which had been early taught and long forgotten, will come back to the memory. They will guard the exercised minds of young Christians from enthusiastic errors into which they are so prone to fall.

It was with extraordinary foresight that the Assembly of Divines at Westminster prepared two different catechisms. The longer of the two was highly approved, but was considered too long to be memorized by children. The Divines then prepared a second, shorter catechism. This contains the substance and even much of the language of the larger version. For centuries then, as a result, children have been able to learn and recite spiritual truths of Scripture.

Although this practice seems to have fallen into almost complete disuse, children who learn true catechisms acquire a treasure more valuable than silver and gold. A child armed with this broad overview of divine truth will not be "carried about with every wind of doctrine," or every wild enthusiasm abroad in the world. When he reads religious books or hears sermons, not only will he understand them better than others do, but he will carry around with him a test for the correctness of what he hears or reads. He will be able to "prove all things, and hold fast to that which is good."

Who should give catechetical instruction? Anyone who can teach divine truth correctly. It is especially the duty of parents, elders and ministers. We can speak strongly in favor of Sunday Schools that give instruction out of the Bible and the catechism.

A church's pastor must have a deep and lively interest in this important exercise. If he is indifferent, no great good will come of it. But if he takes pains to see that classes are fresh and interesting. . . if, like any good teacher, he will propose discussion and inquiry and refer students to good books on the subject, . . . and if he will discuss these important matters freely with young people, he will excite a new spirit of investigation and pursuit of religious knowledge.

If our schools were what they ought to be, seminaries in which Christian doctrine was carefully taught, then our teachers would all be catechists. Children would be trained in the knowledge of God and their duties.

As things stand, this is an appropriate duty of the elders of the church. As leaders of the people, elders should go before them in religious instruction. Every elder should have a little charge of his own to look after, families he should frequently visit and catechize.

If ruling elders are not up to this task, they are unfit for the office which they hold, and can be of little service otherwise to the church.

It is now a common complaint that our elders are not well qualified to perform their duties. How can this evil be remedied? Surprisingly, by simply doing their duty: teaching the doctrines of the church. Mostly by this means they will acquire a taste and thirst for truth, and soon theirs and the church's fund of sound theology will grow.

In the meantime, let pastors meet weekly with their elders for the sole purpose of discussing their duties. Soon, those who are serious about faithfully and intelligently fulfilling their office, will become better prepared for their work.

Does proper catechizing take more time from their businesses than elders can afford? This is a reasonable question, and brings us to our previous point: Schools, among Christians, should have as their chief object bringing up children in the knowledge of divine things. Ideally, the proper catechists of the church would be the teachers of these schools. The truth is, parents should set a much higher value on this than they have been accustomed to, and the church should take pains to train such teachers.

The old plan of catechizing was not confined to children; it was extended to all within the church except officers. Catechizing usually ends too soon, though, and its successes often end with it. Children of 12 or 14 may think they are too big and too old to repeat the catechism.

We are warm friends to instruction in the truths of God's word, and believe that at this most important time of their lives, a combination of extended catechetical instruction and Bible classes are valuable. Who is there who doesn't have more to learn from both? And what on earth is so worthy of time and effort as the knowledge of God's word?

Finally, let all whom God has entrusted with the talent of writing well on theology, take heed to not hide it in a napkin or bury it in the earth. Never was there a time when there was greater need of good thinking and writing to counteract the floods of error, which are coming now from a thousand sources.

Never was there a time when the effect of good writing was so extensive.

By unprecedented means we have opportunity to circulate truth and opinion throughout the world. If godly men sleep, there is no doubt that the enemy will sow his tares plentifully.

Let the friends of truth, therefore, be watchful and wise, and on the alert to seize opportunities to enlighten the world with the pure doctrines of the word of God.

Archibald Alexander, 1837